praise for RICHARD JACKSON

Richard Jackson has extended both the noble body of contemporary poetry as well as its planetary horizons. His lyric sensitivity resembles the smooth flow of a deep river. The surface reflects quotidian events from touching emotions and inspiring landscapes to horrific political crimes but deeper down there the real Dantean drama draws one in the abyss of Promethean empathy and powerful ethical dimensions. His is the poetic beauty and the subtle touch of a man of incredible poetic expression and planetary conscience.

IZTOK OSOJNIK

Richard Jackson has become one of our most important poets. His subjects are those for which poetry originally came into being. The essentials are his songs, his precepts, his adoration, his companions. It isn't any simple solace he offers, but it's solace nevertheless that he lends us.

JAMES TATE

I think he is either Hermes or a Sorrow. He is certainly a messenger. And what he says is contained in a single word, although it comes out as amazement, anger, joy, sadness in an astounding cascade of images, and a variety of tongues. He is a poet of great sweep and vision. He is a master of music; one of our finest poets.

GERALD STERN

He is a kind of Scorsese in poetry, but where Scorsese almost succeeds in his films, then stops, seals and terrifies us, Jackson adds a tender, vulnerable voice that blossoms and transforms us and that is so unique and great, great in its truest sense in Richard Jackson's poems.

TOMAŽ ŠALAMUN

The moths settle on the windowpane:
Small pale telegrams from the world.

TOMAS TRANSTRÖMER
Lament

But speaking the truth in love. . . .

Ephesians 4:15

RETRIEVALS

Richard Jackson

C&R PRESS

C R PRESS

FIRST EDITION PAPERBACK

ISBN-13: 978-1-936196-48-7
ISBN-10: 1-936196-48-4
LCCN: 2014943291

The cover is based upon a wood engraving that
first appeared in Camille Flammarion's 1888
L'atmosphère: Météorologie Populaire.
The artist is unknown.

Book interior & cover design
by Terrence Chouinard
wingwheel.com

I

II

V

to my wife, Terri

I

What are we, in our dream of each other, but a picture which is
The masterpiece of a painter that never painted at all?

FERNANDO PESSOA
Silent Streams

Identity

I. YOUR NAME IN MY NOTEBOOK

As if looking through a pawnshop window at something
you left but can't buy back. Like your name in this notebook
I opened and which I had forgotten. We always leave
these bits of ourselves in another tense. Dusk crowds out
the light. It's like a thread that keeps unraveling until
the sleeve disappears. Or threads of smoke disappearing
above the squatters' shacks by the river. Or the writing of
the mystics that fades into their pages. True, some emotions
seem born on the gallows. I, however, take heart with
Heraclitus who said that the road down and the road up is
the same road. It's like finding a key in the street. The owl
questioning your identity. The window that brings you
the reflection of a stranger. What a relief just to be
someone else for a while! Tonight the moon is a clock
that refuses to work. Why do I feel such happiness
that there is a new dictionary of Mesopotamian languages
that no one can speak? What didn't I say? It was like
the blind man who dealt cards to the neighborhood kids.
Days dawned without permission. I remember our shadows
intersecting on the ground in front of us. The river kept
doing what rivers do which is to hide where they came from.
Flowers spread then without apology over the autumn fields.

II. YOU

Some days I am absolutely convinced you are real.
The headlight flash on the window, the wavering
shadow whose source is out of sight, the odd sound
that has no source. Then it seemed like someone was
knocking at the door. A scratch from a darkened room.
Some days you exist like the last speaker of an extinct
language. These are the silences that litter the heart.
Sometimes I think reality sleepwalks through my dreams.
Too much of what we should have said ends up
in the soul's dead letter office. Too often we follow
forgotten paths. We have to triangulate our position.
There now, I've gone too far and have to turn back.
What I say next depends on who and if you are.
At first all this seemed important, then it didn't.
The place we are is the place we want to be, I thought
you said. The first morning light slaps against the wall.

III. CAMPFIRE

Is what we see trying to hide or trying to escape?
It is as if, by staring, we could know the secrets
no one has suspected were secrets. Or there is
really nothing there but what we create. We want
to rise the way fire does into the purity of air.
For Rilke, pure love meant being consumed in flame.
Dante's lovers spoke through whirlwinds of fire.
What we see and what we love is always disappearing.
The slow smokeless burning of decay is how Frost
described it. What we love when we love each other are
these shapes that keep turning into each other.
Around the campfire, no one speaks. The silence
burns whatever words someone might have said.
The best fires make the least smoke, the most heat.
It's in those flames that our dreams become our own.
Someone pokes a log and the embers fly into another
world. They stare back like the eyes of someone
I had forgotten, someone who hasn't forgotten me.

The Trail

When do you realize the selves you left behind
have gone on without you, living the many lives
you now begin to resemble? So the day hesitates
as if caught in headlights. So the words you write
seem like nonsense someone left on your desk.
The trees pretend to be listening. The owl cares less
who you are. If you are lucky there's a single word
you can take refuge behind. It seems there is
something happening of great importance but
the heart's trail guide herself is lost. Almost invisible,
the ants carry bits of leaf twice their weight
back to the nest. The warning squirrels won't stop
warning. Then you see that what you have written
are wrong directions, scribbled in a language
of condolences, but unable to apologize, missing
the pronouns, missing a destination, missing yourself.

Shorelines

Nobody sees what the other person sees. As when
you pick up at a piece of driftwood and it is not driftwood,
it is the forgotten place it came from. Or when
your dreams wander along the shoreline and your words
no longer believe the things they refer to. I don't
remember why we were there or why we found ourselves
on opposite shores. What drifted in between us were
images I saw once of bodies piled on another shore
by the child soldiers of Kony in Rwanda. The heart is
criss-crossed by these lines. You want me to say
the driftwood symbolizes something. It doesn't.
In a little while the moon will rise on its stem of light
as it always does. The sky will hoard a few stars.
The insects will try to talk to them. You have to know
the difference between the sound of a planet and
the sound of a star. The owl pretends it doesn't care
if you hear him. What I want you to see is that this is
a love poem. It only exists if you see it that way.

The Chair in the Forest

The story begins with the muffled hum of bees you can't see
as they circle a nest in the cushions. It begins with their sound
that folds the air into bolts of cloth. It begins with the whine
of the truck half a mile away on the nearest road. It begins
when we live in the absent sounds of someone else's dreams.
They have gone where they had to go. The sunlight strikes
where it wants to go. There was never any money to stuff into
the cushions. The felled trees have their own stories but are
of no interest here. The path to the next clearing has not been
told yet. Pascal was right, there is no center or circumference.
The bees are souls. The bees wander off. The story begins there.

for Mark Cox

Taking Aim

FROM A PHOTO OF MYSELF WITH RIFLE, 8 YEARS OLD

That's when a bird flies out of the heart, out of memory.
What we see depends on who we are. Only things
that seem to have no meaning gather meaning later on.
Debris lifts the land an average of 4.7 feet each century.
A ton of micrometeorite dust falls to earth every hour.
Who we are depends on what we see. Everything
deepens. The morning paper shows two turtles from
the Eocene era frozen in an act of love, victims of
some poison volcanic ash. What I was is no longer
what I was. What are any of us aiming at? What was I?
What we are on one side of the lens changes who we are
on the other. A chance photo my father took. In a moment
I was no longer what I will be. Don't we want to transcend
the self that can't be transcended? Sometimes we exist
before we exist, but not after. The future is not the future
once you think of it. Sometimes we invent a self we can
talk to. Sometimes I think the wind is blowing backwards.

Škocjan, Slovenia

Something steals the sound of the river filling
the caverns beneath the town. A few voices
guard the cliffs. We want to give these sounds
a meaning they don't have. Even the words here
seem made of stone. And the stones are dreaming
of wings. There's a fault line running through
the church like a memory of the prehistoric town.
The huge gouges in the earth here were once caves.
Someone is still smoking behind a wall where
the village women tend their gardens in the sinkholes
they call *dolina* that were once ancient burial sites.
There are depths here you can only measure by time.
The light stammers. In a while I'll be able to smell
the stars. A wisp of smoke rises like an accusation.
Then suddenly a voice calls as if from the past,
an unwanted memory dives with the falcons out of sight.

for Iztok Osojnik

Ruins

CONVENT, LISBON

If we trace everything back to the Big Bang then we return
to the emptiness we'll become. In Siberia they have uncovered
the bones of the Denisovans who no one can explain but who were
related to humans. In the end we have to believe in ourselves.
The clouds roll up like ancient scrolls. Too often the ruins
we leave behind are not enough. Even the sky becomes a dungeon.
Though everything seems to wait—the road for a traveler,
a leaf for its tree, a ring for the phone to be answered,
there's nothing that will bring us back to what we were.
The sluice gates of horror keep opening like the daily paper,—
as with the story of the tortured girl, how they placed a live rat
in her vagina, and there is none—no response—that makes
any sense now, though I want to think our words must be empty
in order to be filled, I want to stop these shadows from shivering
behind me, I want to forget the news that's flooding the airways
with an image of our days, —the child born without a brain,
his head a collapsed balloon, his stars long ago become dust,
his sky tortured, my own words trying desperately to fill my lungs.

Petroglyph Hands

CANYON DE CHELLY, ARIZONA

Sometimes we push so hard into the earth we leave
The hand print of desire. Without rocks there is no soul.
So many figures keep disappearing into the earth.
The wind against the rocks is not the wind. It is
Spirit. The rocks wear it like a skin. You can hear
the voice of the slaughtered in the light that echoes
from 1805 and the other end of the canyon. It has
come a long way to touch us. The sound of the flute
player and the man who dances to that silent music
or is stunned into silence at our own ignorance
show how dangerous it is to love the earth. Sometimes
the dust picks up and the hands sift its memories.
When was it we first needed words to touch each other?

Volunteers

It was our belief that all roads lead somewhere
that was our downfall. In fact, everyone was leading
a life hidden from themselves. Meteors skim by,
stars explode, graveyards are grown over. I struggle,
now, just to describe the smell of rain on asphalt
that still carries me, after all these years, to a place
I can't identify. There was a boy back then burned
from fresh road tar. Another who fell from the roof
we used to climb. I still can't figure out how they are
related. History takes care of itself despite our attempts
at revision. In the end it isn't hard to abandon truth's
training wheels. It's love, after all that takes us
where we want to go, and every love is more than
its love, like those *volunteers*, you call them, that grow
unexpectedly from seeds you buried in the compost,
arriving, as it were, from nowhere we needed to identify.

for Terri

Numbers

There are so many ways to measure what we want.
There are 400 steps to the temple of the 10,000 Buddhas.
In 1789 Herschel described the heavens as an endless
garden of Eden. Here the gardens seem to rise from
those 10,000 minds. Each of the Buddhas has a singular
personality. Incense folds itself into intricate layers
of cloud. For a moment we become whatever watches us.
How many angels on the head of a pin, they used to ask.
How many. . . some of those old jokes began. But here
all 10,000 are one. In every eye another eye is watching.
The heart beats 100,000 times a day. That means there's
enough time to love everyone. We circle the Milky Way
every 200 million years. The number of colors you see
in the spectrum depends on what you were taught. Some
mega churches measure faith by the number of parishioners.
The Buddha says enlightenment cannot be measured.
Statistics say I'll live to 80. Rats can have sex 60 times
a day—which is a cause for extreme joy or jealousy.

Confessional

The mountains seem to hover over the mist.
The river is filled with absence. Spiders fling
their silk out to far branches with abandon.
It is so easy to be trapped by what you say.
The shadows the crow casts as it flies over
seem more real than the crow. The early light is
nearly undecipherable. What is the name
of that insect that devours its mate?
The hour is less compliant than it used to be.
This Fall the whole tree is learning how to
translate eternity. The right words hardly
ever arrive on time. The treaty arrives after
too many people have died. In Central Congo
they simply hack off limbs. The mist on this page is
not burning off. Doesn't everyone do something
they won't confess to? The worst atrocities
start with the smallest transgressions. The river
has no idea there is an ocean at its end. You have
to write words that aren't afraid of listening.

for Michael Panori

Butterflies

All the energy collected by radio telescopes since
they started is only equal to the energy of a butterfly
landing on a flower. Which is to say how little we know
about what is in our own solar system, or ourselves.
In fact, Pluto's orbit is so irregular we don't know where
it will appear next. Which is how, I suppose, you have
landed here in this sentence and, like gravity, have begun
to shift the focus. Maybe that's why I think of Newton,
who, poisoned by Mercury from his alchemy experiments,
couldn't remember where he put his proofs for elliptical
orbits. There's no reality without its proof, Halley had argued
years before the comet was named for him. The energy
it takes to remember is the energy it takes to love,
the saying goes, taking so little, as those butterflies know,
to flutter and fly off because there is no formula, and
because love is stronger than the proofs we remember for it.

for Pam & Bill

Desperate Note from Byron's Palace in Lerici

In the blue wind the leaves begin to think they are birds.
This is when you lean your body against its sorrows.
The truth is always there with its hidden reefs.
Your touch still hovers over the shore. Each wave is
a mirror that washes in a past we wanted hidden.
Now our voices are roosting in the branches.
Everything is echo, or shadow. Your shadow
walking on the other side of the street, your shadow
sitting in a passing car, your last words casting
the shadow that has replaced my own. Where have
we been that has brought us here? The past burrows
into me like an insect. The tree frogs, after tonight's
rain, fill the woods. They throw their voices
so predators can't find them. The old truths are
falling from the branches. The old dreams wash up
on the shores of our souls. Sometimes I think
the soul is a shadow even gravity can't touch,
and love is what passes in the mirror as we look away.

for Gerald Stern

Pigeons

A flap of wings brings us together for a moment.
My father, his mind flown, could only point.
It was a sound like the closing of many books.
I remember a rusty moon that would later rise.
Inside a turtle's shell, an enormous silence.
Under its stars it is hard to know what to feel.
The heart has so many empty cabinets.
Shadows have so many objects to account for.
The sky never gets tired of being the sky.
All sorts of birds have disappeared there.
The only word we said was never uttered.

Tree with Moon

Someone says the tree is in a good mood tonight.

There's no message it feels obligated to give.

Even the moon has no desire to break through.

Tonight I can believe everything no one else does.

What does it matter who dies in Syria or Lebanon?

In the next lot the raccoons are doing what they always do.

The memory of things becomes the reality of things.

Or maybe the past is not permanent. Maybe the tree has

said its fill, and leaves us with an image of ourselves.

The Invisible Object

Everything happens just over the horizon. That way
we can claim to have no influence. We say the same
thing about the dark. Our words are like flashlight
beams of searchers poking their wands in the woods.
How easy it is to lose track of it before you know
you have it. I am surprised now and then to see anything
that matters. I can't tell whether the voices are
coming closer or drifting away into the troubled clouds.
The future is shivering in the next few lines.
Whatever it was has disappeared into another
plot. Even its name is a secret. At this point I'd settle
for anything—a woman's silk glove, rusty harmonica,
lost key, empty diary. My own heart seems
locked away, the combinations lost, tomorrow lost
among the endless echoes of words not yet spoken.

for Gary Margolis

II

While the sweet breath of heaven
Was blowing on my body, [I] felt within
A correspondent breeze, that gently moved
With quickening virtue, but is now become
A tempest, a redundant energy,
Vexing its own creation.

WILLIAM WORDSWORTH
The Prelude

Flood Stage

I can hear that bird again who doesn't understand the huge
dungeon the sky has become. Maybe it is trying to escape
our torrent of newsreel horrors. Maybe it thinks it could
save us like Noah's raven or dove. Rows of corn have flooded
and the fields bare their souls to the sky. The river's rising.
Sometimes the bloated bodies of animals pass by, but these are
nothing compared to what has been haunting me today,
the bloated bodies of children left as a sign by the Somalian
Al-Shabaab who deny the drought, who refuse aid from
the west. In the end, can't we just believe in ourselves?
Sometimes the incalculable detritus of the stars falls
around us, and we no longer read the pleas of the dove,
the heart's evidence, the ravens that haunt mass graves of Srebenica,
the Congolese women raped by soldiers in North Kivu Provence.
Sometimes I think morning is there just to try wringing the last
drops of darkness from the sky. Sometimes the sandbags we live
behind are not enough, the sluice gates of horror keep opening.
But today, today I just want to forget the news that's flooding
the airways with an image of our days, the child born without
a brain, his head a collapsed balloon, his stars long ago drowned,
his sky tortured, beliefs floundering, my own words trying
desperately to drown in meanings that make no sense.

for David Rivard

Happelings

I. WHEN IT HAPPENS

Maybe as you come around the corner to meet someone
or start to leave the store overloaded with your groceries,
and maybe you notice the shadows stalking the hour
or the disguises of trees, maybe even the man holding
the cardboard sign asking for gas money. Maybe it's
the way the moon gambles with the streetlights, or
the wind conspires with the litter. In a moment you think
you are looking through a madhouse mirror. There must be
something you can do but even the clouds are filled with
indecision. Still there's the child with the bullet in his head
and the others strewn around the ball court. The sky
complains, buildings lean away, pigeons mumble.
Sometimes our words scatter off like roadside crows.
Already the windows are tired of letting death peer though them.

II. HOW IT HAPPENED

It was a time when their hopes occupied the museums.
Even the planets just couldn't seem to get oriented.
There were too many unplotted consequences. Before
they knew it the old subjects were no longer valid,
not even usable. Strange signs began to appear on
the horizon but they had faith some meanings would
follow. Despite the reports from arbitrary villages.
Birds scattered at the warning sounds no one else heard.
Everyone tried to keep a light burning inside them.
The weather saddened. The roads grew dizzy. It was
a time when the stars looked to the village for guidance.
No one asked why the spiders' webs disappeared
each morning. Tracks were always being swept over.
The boys playing in the first crater never heard the click
that froze their words mid air without any meaning.

Abandoned

KING'S CHAPEL ABANDONED GRAVEYARD, ALABAMA

Eternity dies here. The light turns dry. Invisible insects
sway the grass as if there were a breeze. A butterfly
steals from a flower and is gone. What marks us at
the end are approximations, spaces emptied of all
we were. I want the secret names we carry to be
written here. I want the light stored in the leaves
to be released, the dark hiding in roots to surface.
The song of a Bachman's Sparrow tries to extend
beyond its own ending as it echoes itself desperately.
The shadows wander, restless. The chapel long ago
turned back into earth. Whoever once marked
these graves has wandered off into the silences
beyond the woods. Inside us, everything has
fallen asleep. What I want is the soul of something
buried deep inside me before it became these words.

Bird

Breath fills the decayed tree. The sky is still
a syllable. Light lives inside those wings. We have
no word to describe the insects' tremors beneath
the bark, or to measure the currents between here
and the next tree. What do we know? The night
won't *fall* as we like to say, and I'll wait till
the last star introduces itself though most of them are
galaxies. What he sees is what we have clear cut
or strip mined. Sunlight steps carefully across
the water. I don't have any words that could
apologize. The ripples make a transcript I can't read.
How often we think of things which are only
our idea about them. The only flowers that speak are
The absent ones. The bird knows each name is
a superstition, each origin has already taken flight,
already landed, invisible, unbearable, trying to sing.

for Jim & Dara

27

At that Hour

An unsuspecting moon was busy somewhere else.
A moth was trapped between two window panes.
There were birds falling that someone took for angels.
Another Sarin attack descended like a poacher's net.
The bodies seemed to be staring at the clouds.
The clouds turned away towards some arbitrary dream.
Distant hills began to melt under the sun.
The shrapnel from their dreams could kill us.
The blueprint for how we should react was stolen.
All of our hopes were tangled in history's roots.
One shadow began to devour another shadow.
The child, you'd think she moved, but it was just the gas.

Bosnian Rhapsody

Night had snuck through the barbed wire perimeter.
Moonlight bled into the surrounding clouds. You could
barter a button for a piece of bread. You could hide
for a long time beneath slogans. If you just change
the place not much has changed. Sometimes the shadows
of missing relatives wandered the yard. The men stood
around in clouds made of breath. There were many
unused rooms in their hearts. Here the sky is hopelessly
lost. We get the news from one reliable source, or another.
Truth holds on like a flood survivor on a rooftop.
There, the most important words were given new meanings.
Tattered shadows were weighed down by stories no one
believed. Flood lights stalked the fences. At every horizon
history waited to speak. The path a bullet takes stays frozen
in the air for decades. The whole story could be told today
by the young boy kicking a ball across the yard that is
no longer there. Under the stones beyond the camp
there are still stories that think they have escaped.

Lidice

They are looking at a town made from splinters of memory.
On the opposite hill, only a marker where the church stood,
where the few birds seem to crawl across the sky. If you
think about death long enough it begins to think about you.
The land here refuses any tracks. The wind gropes at the past.
Even now their gaze is vulnerable though the Nazis have left
decades ago. A whole town that no longer had a name on a map.
It's as if these children have returned from the camps alive.
Sometimes your memories return to the window to gaze at you.
What they are asking is that we find a way to love one another,
to find some whiff of God in the air. There are words but
no language for what happened here. What they understand is
the way the pearl gives the oyster its troubling dreams.

The Bone Church

CZECH REPUBLIC

After a while it doesn't matter whose bones are
crossed with yours. We are what we are becoming
a part of. And before the drawn breath before the first
word that names us. There's a small lizard that disappeared
behind a skull. That too. There are 400 miles of blood
vessels in the brain, 100 billion neurons. Lin Zhao in prison
for 20 years wrote everything in his own blood. All those
sense impressions, all those feelings, where do they go
when we do? Wycliff's bones were exhumed after twenty
 years and burned at the stake for heresy. Paleolithic
peoples emptied the brains from skulls then buried
the skulls in the center of stone circles to receive the tribe's
new dreams. What do the characters in my poems dream
when I look away? Each dream is the lie of another dream.
Each of these selves dreamt of being other selves, other bones.
Only in imagining a thing does it become real, as Ezekiel
said. After a while I even believe it is me writing this poem.
Only in silence do we hear what we need to hear.

The Eyes

What the eye holds is wilder than we admit.
No one knows the darkness we harbor there.
The soul quivers in its den. Bats ruffle
their wings. They are waiting for a sign
that promises a world reshaped by sound.
I stop short inside this dream of dreaming.
I remember my father sleeping with one eye
open. We have to see through, not with
the eye, wrote Blake. What the eye emits,
wrote Berkley, is all that there is. And what
could seem emptier than the sky despite
the constant birth of stars and galaxies.
Some of the bats are dying from a white
fungus that spreads behind the brow of
their cave like a wrong thought. What is
reflected in the eye is a den of dreams.
We hardly notice what lens we see through,
but in every eye another eye stalks.

Torture

Sometimes we reduce the world to a single hill, and
the hill to a bombed out farm where a man scours a brick
pile to read his fate. The trouble is, there's nothing there
he wants to believe. The clouds roll up like ancient scrolls
we can't read. Sometimes our lives are tightropes starting
to unravel, and sometimes we want the blind eyes of
the mole who eats the earth. Sometimes our lives are
like the hung body just before the rope snaps, as this morning,
hearing the story of the tortured girl, how they sewed up
her vagina, and, but what can you say after that and not be
dishonest, for any response is a lie, any word that says
you know who you are is a lie, any metaphor is an assault.

Vultures

The only question is which death has attracted them.
How easy it is for the heart to claim each death as
its own. A body out of sight returning to the form
it had before it was a form. That is the fear. At some
point any object becomes any other object. The soul's
tightrope unraveling. Between two words is another word
not spoken, between two breaths the undrawn breath
that defines us. Do I invent you or do you invent me?
Our fears would stop if only we became the fear.
It's the words as much as anything that swoop in on
whatever seems to be different. There needs to be
a ballistics report on those words. What those vultures
sense is something trying to remain itself. What I want is
something so true to itself it no longer resembles itself.

Tank Traps

LJUBLJANA, SLOVENIA, 1992

Someone is watching from the window across the square.
There are night birds complaining as they maneuver
and dive between the lights. We could drink the darkness.
Those aren't child's jacks or crosses as they seemed from afar.
Below us, a Roman city smirks about what we'll never know.
South of here the souls of the dead disguise themselves as
clouds to escape the militia. Each day is another trap.
Our words are blemishes on the truth. Every heart is crossed out.
The darkness provokes a few whispers. Everywhere we look
something crosses our path. We can't see the lovers yet,
about to cross from the right. We can't see the child
crossing out what he's just written. There are no halos
on the streetlights. These designs imprison us. The sky
leans down. If we aren't careful we'll cross out the world.

The Work of Revelation

In a while you'll be gone and our shadows will
become fossils. Sometimes we pluck our lives out
like flowers and let them wilt on the counter, or
leave them by the side of the road like curls
from a truck's blown tire. What's to salvage?
All the stars we see will eventually burn out.
If you don't tend it, the soul molds like bread.
The footpaths wander into the hungry fields.
Our years are like a child's dates on a moss-covered
headstone. Each refusal strips off a layer of the soul.
Not far from here, the poet Kosovel wrote poems
no one would read for forty years. Dying, he could still
watch from this window the sunlight grazing
on the distant hillside fields, the lizards flickering
in the garden, the hawks circling a prey both it and
we will never see, trying to create his own memories
before he left, knowing, even then, how we are all
dying from wounds we never know we have.

The Beach

FROM A PICTURE OF MY FATHER DOING HANDSTANDS, 1955

On the picture are scratches, or shards of light,
the detritus of invisible stars sifting through the clouds.
1950, the world as deadly as it is today what with beliefs
floundering in Somalia, the Congo, Sudan. So there's
my father and two friends doing handstands at Salisbury Beach.
It must be low tide given the distant, thin line of waves
behind them. The sky is wrinkled, the beach almost deserted.
Another war across the sea, Korea. He won't have to go
this time. It's as if their feet were holding up the sky
like caryatids. My father is the one with the shirt.
In twenty years, his brain washed clean, he will remember
only that. Back then he must be thinking the world makes
more sense this way. That's why he's looking away from us.

for Sherry & Brian

37

Thirteen Sentences on the Cave

There are whispers etched on the furthest walls.

There are so many caves within the cave of the self.

Each whisper hangs from another whisper.

The darkness repeats itself to the opening.

Hollowed out by a river that is no longer a river.

Before that, a glacier, and then an inland sea.

There were stars too, but arranged differently.

There are whispers inside us we never hear.

The ones we do hear we don't want to hear.

There are selves we never know except as echoes.

Anything possible already exists, wrote Spinoza.

A darkness that hides the darkness from the dark.

To be whispered, as the wind blows away the wind.

III

To speak from a place where silence speaks.

IZTOK OSOJNIK
Postcards from Hvar

Unsaying: Meditations from Slovenia
I. NEVER THERE
SOČA VALLEY, ISONZO FRONT, 1917

They are hesitant, the buds, barely visible on the lime trees. They seem to know what emptiness they will replace. They seem to know history is a faded watermark. The road collects its own past with each hesitating hairpin turn. We are here as part of an ongoing litany but can't confirm that now. The hawk that watches me suspiciously from a branch above the soldiers' graveyard waits for a mouse to emerge from under the ground cover to reveal itself. Each soldier here knew a moment that stretched one life into another. It always seems to come after the fact. There is no truth, even in that moment. By now the evening that seemed to take forever to begin fills with clouds that tell the first stars to wait, be cautious for what comes next. It is a moment when everything remembers what was never there as something that will always be there.

II. MIXED METAPHORS FOR WHO KNOWS WHAT
RAKOV ŠKOCJAN

The river here grinds down the sandstone into a past we have forgotten and tells a future we'll never know. The natural stone bridges are doorways filled with doorways. These are stories that never resolve themselves on their own. There are no antecedents for the pronouns though we get some picture of where they are headed. Beyond, an unseen town hovers over the ridge where the evergreens stand stark black against a red sky. Someone always expects something of us. The wind is trying to tally the results. We try to read the stars but they don't know anymore than we do. The walls of the cliffs assert traces from epoch to epoch. There's something I want to ask but my words outpace their meanings. That's when the fox drifts out of the woods as if he knew what I was thinking.

III. WORDLESS

MLINO, LAKE BLED

It was a night where there were only words that had no meaning.
At first they semed to float like pollen through the dream. Then
they were stars. Then like the flashlights of searchers lacing through
the woods except there were no woods. No stars or pollen either,
but like them. How long had I lain there? I could almost hear an
owl question the status of certain stars but by then I was waking.
Was he in the dream or in the woods? There was a war and then
there wasn't. The whole place seemed a façade to hide a broken sky.
There are whole lists we are not privy to. The reeds coming out of
the water, I now see, were only a distraction. Someone else stops
on the opposite shore because he hears something. He is made of
the same dream of atoms as I am. His words are taking forever to
reach me. How long has it been? What were the lights searching
for? Then, suddenly, I am older and no longer myself.

IV. TEMPERATURE INVERSION

POSTOJNA

These trees tell us there is no place we are safe. Wind, then ice, have whittled away the tops or decapitated them, cracked them like arthritic bones. But why these metaphors that steal what they try to name and understand? There is a whole realm of being that is beyond them for *whittle, decapitated* and *bones* make them human and hide the loss of light that shaded and formed each leaf or needle, how those drew water to make sap, and how a whole world of nests, worms, insects, bacteria, entangled systems disappeared. We ourselves are metaphors for what we can't do. Trees and ideals collapse. We want a world that is easier to understand. But now these new leaves have not known another life and, regardless of the future, pay no attention to mine or anyone's words for them.

V. THE HIDDEN

CERKNICA, THE DISAPPEARING LAKE

It is all limestone here, porous, where the lake disappears into an-
other world beneath this one like a nest in the hollow of a tree. It is
here even when it isn't. It's a question of belief. Of faith. One time,
as a boy, I tried to hold a shaft of sunlight like a spear that had come
through my bedroom window. What we see is already something
else. After the Big Bang, the universe went dark not even believing
in itself, just bubbles of ionized gas, until the first stars emerged.
That is always the way. Night gathers in pools by the roadside. They
hold within them galaxies of other times and places. It was Jason
and the Argonauts who must have figured the world was shrinking
back into one atom when they visited here. After it didn't, they in-
vented another theory. This is the case with every belief, disappear-
ing into itself, into whatever it is we believe we saw.

VI. MISSING

It is as if you could see the buried city beneath this one the way we
used to look at our bones by holding a light behind our hands, or
the way those old x-ray machines for measuring shoe size revealed a
body we didn't know. Beneath me stirs the Roman town of Emona
where I imagine a blacksmith trying to imagine what dreams we
forge. They don't get any better. An express train drags the past
through the station. The news today is all abduction, shifting bor-
ders and pillage. What we don't know is fast approaching. What we
thought were harmless ideas turned out to be accomplices. The
streetlights are never bright enough. At such times we are all miss-
ing. Sometimes the truth is the nature we hide from ourselves. It
is buried beneath the silt of our words. It is is not the question of
archeology as we had imagined.

VII. HISTORY

The body doesn't know what to do with its discarded feelings. They
stand like broken columns the Romans left just breaking into con-
sciousness above the grass line. In the distance, the moon burrows
into a mountain, the sky turns into earth. In a little while we'll be liv-
ing in the marrow of darkness. They used to think lighthouses were
the answer until pirates lit false fires on the rocks. The heart, some-
one said, is a grifter. We are all dark matter. No one knows where our
stories came from. In the center of town Orpheus' monument is
powerless to resurrect anything. All there is now is his voiceless light.
The ancient trade routes have changed direction. There are too
many erasures here to count. The body knows what beats in the heart
is not the heart but hearts.

IV

On the surface, an intelligible lie; underneath, an unintelligible truth.

MILAN KUNDERA

The Unbearable Lightness of Being

Introduction to Metaphysics

There are some dreams you will never enter though
they go on without you. Their streets have no direction,
their houses have no addresses, streetlights flicker from
one darkness to another, or at least this is what you dream
you have dreamt. Just like the shadow you fear is dreaming
you. It is someone you recognize, someone whose importance
has been lopped off like the branch of the tree outside
your window. There are bags stuffed with old clothing
in the room where you wake. Someone else's phone is
ringing silently. The alarm clock is counting backwards.
They key to it all seems to rest in the octagon coins
you pull from your pocket and which carry your own face,
dirtied like the ominous clouds that have come too close to earth.

Epistemology

They never end, our stories, though we try to tie them neatly
into sentences that yoke together like the aqboxcars I can hear
slamming together in the rail yard to make a single train,
but they always seem to end up in some far flung city whose
name escapes us. The stars assemble on invisible branches
waiting for us to name their shapes and we say *starthistle*
or *sunflower* to link the earth and sky. *True,* we like to say
as a kind of assurance we know what we mean, but it's
a word that has the same root as *truce,* and even *tryst,*
though few of them are based on truth, and, more to the point,
the Old French word *triste,* a place to position yourself
during a hunt, or today, just plain sad. Maybe truth just takes
time to decipher just as a river takes ages to find the bottom of
the gorge, or the way a moth once thought its pupa was
a galaxy. And here, —so much lies beyond the words
we do find: *cat's ear, horseweed, rattlesnake, goosegrass,*
doveweed, skunk cabbage, crowfoot, names that suggest
animals whose death has resurrected them as plants.
Tonight, I learned a name for our native grass: *lovegrass,*
wind dancer, what the Cherokee called it, and wondered
how many names are waiting to tell our own story.

for Chris Buckley

The Voices

I. THE GIFT

This plastic cup with the broken handle, green enough to
almost disappear in the grass by the roadside, has come
all the way from its origins in oil, and so it may be the last
gesture of some dinosaur or hold the last breath of an ancient
fern. About the size of a fist, it may have been tossed out
a window, probably from a muscle car, perhaps thrown
in disgust at what was said on the radio news, or held
some bourbon before the driver spotted the police
cruiser behind him. Had he lost his job? Had his wife
left him for his best friend? It hasn't been here long.
The crows are busy with what's been pasted to the road.
Greasy wrappers, newspaper, even a used diaper
tell their own stories. The cup's probably made in China,
probably by some worker not paid enough to buy it.
Certainly the boys on the county clean-up detail would have
bagged it had they passed this way. If I leave it, perhaps
a mouse or an insect will make a home. We all need a home.
Just into the tree line the homeless tent village stays
out of sight. Someone there could use it. Maybe the one
who will thumb his way to Georgia for the onion harvest.
Or I could simply take it home to use as a planter to hold
the miniature, flowerless cactus my wife had left for me.

II. TRACKS

It's not the thing but its hollowed shape. You have to
think not of what's there but what isn't there. You look
for what side has crumbled and what the spacing is
if you want to know where it was going and how fast.
Everything has a story. It was leaping towards
a thicket, the two oval-shaped impressions spread
a bit for each foot, making distance, as they say,
from the rifle's search. No other tracks, he was alone.
There's ghostly mist lowing from the trees. The leaves
kicked up say it was panic. A few hours old, there is
no other sign. He could be watching. He could be
on the other side of the ridge. We all have something
that pursues us. Tracks tell us only what they want to.
Every vision wants to be more than it is. The signs
we read are not the ones we need. What Jesus wrote
in the sand was not words but the mind's struggle
to enter its own vision. Every sign holds a memory
for what we were or what we will become. The same
mist seems to be falling over and over again. It leaves
no tracks except to tell us we are here, we are alone.

III. WATERFALL

I might as well begin by saying the river is not
the symbol you think it is. Nothing to do with
the history it carries, the prophecy it becomes,
nothing to do with the dreams that catch in branches
on the falls. There's one tree that resists going over but
it won't be long. Heraclitus was right—everything
disappears. It is like having too many ideas to sort
a meaning from. Sometimes you can't tell the water's
reflection of trees from the trees. Everything fits
into an equation for which no one has intended
an answer. Should I have focused on the mist
that hovers over whatever is lost? Where upstream
a capsized canoe begins the story of three lives
that have joined the flotsam of memory? What
about the family posing there for a camera who know
nothing of this? Our lives are shoe boxes of old
pictures. At most a few tattered edges on a wallet photo.
What else is there but our words that cut through water
and leave a wake we pretend, sometimes, is meaning?

Not Said

Gravity happens to the lens. Words squint but
it doesn't help. I want the mailman to deliver
another story. Instead there are only the homeless
men washing the windshield for a quarter. Why
does love seem stuffed in the trunk? This is not
a calculus problem. The bridge from here
to there hasn't been delivered. Empty bullet
casings litter the scene. No one is ever a witness.
The heart sags. My footprints forget me.
I don't think anything will ever be the same.
This is the edge of the cliff and you can't move,
can't jump. Everything is vertical. With binoculars
you can see where you'll be in an hour. Raindrops
collect on the lens. A fine mist. It hides us.
It drifts into clocks. Gravity presses your hands.
Some hurts never get said. Some get smuggled.

The Truth

It's true, the shortest distance between two points is
not always a straight line. Nor between each of us.
It's true, our words feel too light, and even Einstein
doesn't make any sense. What is the shape of love?
We can see it only by distant lightning flashes. But
it's not gravity that holds our hearts inside our chests.
There's a whole world that lives outside our mirrors.
It's true we have to choose between parallel universes.
In one universe the flowers forgive a trapped love.
In another they scourge the air we breathe.
One village has its hands cut off.
Another scavenges for air-dropped food.
We make our walls out of our fears, it's true,
but we have to decide if it is to keep love out or in.
It is true, the wind is stuttering in the trees.
It is true, the tracks of the fox outdistance its life.
We have to choose if the river's bones show
where the river falls or where it will flood again.
These are signs we can read however we want.
Here are my shoes filling with tomorrow.
Here are my syllables turning to pure air,
speaking a language that is all disguise. It is true,
in Ezekiel's valley of dry bones it is the wind,
the breath of souls, that brings new life
whenever we choose to love the worlds we make.

for Brett Lott

The Rapids

The river we have inside us suspects the truth.
That Life began, as Lucretius said, by inheriting itself.
That everything just changed from one kind of atom
to another. This is a belief that Hypatia of Alexandria was
flayed alive for. Now the light thickens. The water is
deeper than it seems. We know what our words mean
by what flows over them. That's why they keep changing
before we can say them. Does the river remember
the rocks it grinds into sand? The shape of the river is
a question asked miles upstream. Language is fossil poetry,
wrote Emerson. What was left of the famous library
in Alexandria was burned by Calef Omar. No one knows
what happened to the 113 lost plays of Sophocles.
Sometimes, though, you can hear what the river has
brought to us. When we try to fathom any of this we are
talking about the depth of two outstretched arms,
about six feet, or about the average depth of a grave.
This is why the first philosophy, as they say, was about
indigestion. To Philosophize is to learn to die, wrote Montaigne.

Roots

The way the brain's ganglia disappear into folds of tissue
just as truth always hides from us like the way we can see
only 2,000 of the billions of stars out there with the naked eye,
too much, like the way I am trying to stop this series now as
each image disappears like one of those faces on post office walls,
or the way the Nile seemed to disappear for those early explorers
though some thought its source was in the mountains of the moon
or, for some who thought they could dig their way through
the earth to China, there, which is what Dante seemed to do
when he emerged upside down at Mount Purgatory, or even
that lost boy in that 1950's movie, the mine shaft threatening
to collapse on him like his birthday cake should he ever see it,
unlike the mules in the Dixson mine in Dayton, Tennessee,
who never left, and remained blind, not worrying about where
they might go next, rooted as we often are, to a single point of view.

The Dancing Building, Prague

There is no one shape for truth. It used to be
you could see it in the outline of a winter tree
against the sky. Now the pigeons carry bits of broken
dreams away, the windows fill with questions
we never hear. In one room an artist fails to paint
his ghosts, in another a clerk keeps erasing his own
name. Sooner or later an answer leans over to whisper.
One time it was 1954, the rapids twisting down
the flume. What did it matter if we didn't understand?
It was about balance. It was about the way sunlight,
for one irretrievable moment, makes everything dance.
A truth caught with its mouth open. The sky tilting
away forever. It is like imagining the dead visit you
and then mistake you, they believe this, for one of them.

Soundings

HUMPBACK WHALE OFF NEW ENGLAND COAST

What we know deeply we know for such a short
time before it appears again, distant and foreign.
Where do our words go once they are spoken?
The whale sheaths itself and leaves behind a footprint
of oil. The sea gathers the setting light of the sky.
At some point, the sea becomes the sky.
This is what Jonah had to learn, that it is
all loneliness, all forgiveness, all gathering
from the puzzling depths he carried within him.
Above, a gull dives into a cloud. An invisible
plane leaves a vapor trail the wind bends. There is
a kind of truth we only see when we close our eyes.

for Nancy

Despair

TO THE MAN ON THE STEPS, MARYLAND

So much of what we dream flickers out before we can
name it. Even the sun has been frozen on the next street.
Every word only reveals a past that never seems real.
Sometimes we just stare at the ground as if it were
a grave we could rent for a while. Sometimes we don't
understand how all that grief fits beside us on the stoop.
There should be some sort of metaphor that lifts us away.
We should see the sky open up or the stars descend.
There are birds migrating, but we don't hear them, cars
on their way to futures made of a throw of the dice.
The pigeons here bring no messages. A few flies
stitch the air. Sometimes a poem knows no way out
unless truth becomes just a homeless character in it.

Faith in Romania

It must be the child has turned to call us to follow.
The cart is filled with the harvest. Ahead of them
the road can't decide between harvest and planting.
The camera has refused to read an invisible dust
that rises like prayer. They are headed towards mounds
that are man's early attempts to reach heaven.
A hidden road turns left. Not yet dusk but already
the stars are waiting to drink the darkness.
My gaze here stumbles through lost centuries.
The early moon behind me pretends it is a clock.
They could be heading to Emmaus or Egypt.
What they seek is what we find in them.
We are all prisoners of our own happiness.

In the Space Below, Explain Any Extenuating Circumstances

The sun passed overhead on a stretcher.

It didn't matter how many words we hurled

against the door. All our hopes floated to the surface

of the water. It didn't matter how many rocks

we threw against the hour. Time curdled in the pails.

Every touch is a threshold to some other world,

some indecipherable constellation that seems to hang in front of you.

Every time we turn away a whole universe gets swept

under the rug. Spiders thrive behind the stove.

There are letters I've written that have no words yet.

There are feelings that blossom like poppies and sound

like violins of light. Sometimes you look into

a distance so deep your eyes smolder.

In that distance I can see the freight trains carry your hopes

to places you can hardly imagine.

These are the trains that chip away the darkness.

Leap

MARBLEHEAD, MASSACHUSETTS

You have to believe as a character in an abandoned draft
believes. The way those boys jump spread-eagled from
the trestle. From one phrase into the empty space erased
by another phrase. A wave crumpled against the side of
a bridge. The waterfall desperate to fill the pool at its base.
All those dead bees caught in the honey pot. The story
invents you. A tidal river that could pull you back to sea.
The name of every question being chance or risk. There's
an answer that refuses to be written despite my best
efforts. The train hasn't passed over the trestle in decades.

Magritte's *Human Condition*

PRETTY RIVER RETREAT, MISSOURI

Behind every world another one waits, scrambling

to get out of the frame. No one is going to

claim any tree is real, or any cloud knows where

it is going. Where we are is the barren room

the artist abandoned. That too is a world in need

of another. Behind it I imagine you will be

waiting if only I could find the right word for you.

But who else's name whistles through

the trees, who else's heart dives with the eagle

into the lake? Our words are the easels

we have forgotten. We have to speak beyond

the words we paint, beyond the silence

that is the forest of stars drowning in the water.

V

In the murk of our darkness, you, Epicurus, raised your blazing
lantern to show us the blessings of life.

Titus Lucretius Carus
On the Nature of Things

Fog

Crows and elephants watch over their dead and mourn.
How strange to come back now to that sentence, weeks
later. It's almost time to leave. Every sound is louder
in the fog. My watch strains to go backwards. Shadows whisper
where no shadows could be. An echo of the moon strays
out of the last ruins of darkness. Yes, the two men in the boat
about to become fog are real. So, too, the dreams that are
lost among the fallen trees that scratch the shoreline.
Last night, the stars on the water were trap doors. The crows
with their charred wings are complaining to a hawk. It's time
to pack up the sunsets, the dawns and move on. There's our dog
sniffing below this window who knows everything else we can't see.

Spider Web

We are mostly what we don't understand,
we are mostly like gulls following trawlers into
port. A few boys practicing their aim there
at abandoned factory windows, a family
living in a rusted Dodge, a baby left on a church
step, just another day. The future plays its cards
close to the chest. But sometimes, unexpectedly,
you catch a stranger's eye on the street and it
reveals the need for mystery. Which is why,
in all this, I believe the chalk drawings children
leave on the sidewalk are the only clues we have
to save one another. Which is why my metaphor is
the web's dew shaking the moonlight that refuses
to be trapped and rolled up for later use, refuses.

Symbols

For some of us there is only the shadow we step behind
that turns always into night, a night that leaves no memory.
Its galaxies constantly change shape because of the weight
of dark matter. This too is only a question of belief. For us,
there is no difference between the moon and its reflection.
The earth releases the song of the sky. Clouds slip
between our fingers. A rag of dust sweeps across the street
and someone will always follow it. Our steps have no roots.
There is always this horizon that sleeps in our words.
There is always another direction, another symbol to read.
Dust, cloud, darkness, so many ways to lose our way.
There is always the irrefutable abyss we fill with love.

Diaspora

To say this is just another poem about the moon would be
a lie. To say anything you have to know the angle of
the sky. I mean, the footprints of the sky. They appear
as if they were crows. It was Plato who said we are birds
without feathers. The sky flutters. Constellations are closed.
Telescopes are useless. The big truths are always echoes
or reflections. That's why it is so easy to get your sources
mixed up. We see by a grizzled light. In Nigeria lies
flock to the jungle. The moon takes pity on the lake.
But that doesn't matter because the moon is not
the subject here. Who absconded with the truth?
There are tiny insects eating the paper of ancient books.
They aren't any smarter, but neither are we. Leopardi
used dozens of words to described the moon. Now
it just sits there not saying a thing. The crows sit on
the telephone line but hear nothing, as if they were waiting
for their execution. They are silhouetted against the moon.
Its light is a form of diaspora but from where we don't know.

for Mary Ruefle

Cumberland Island

The live oak elbows its branches into the ground
to imitate our lives. Swallows carry messages
from last souls. Some dreams never fly off, some
never sleep. Shawls of moss hang from the branches.
They lull you. The moon pushes up on a stem of light
over the horizon. The earth floats in its air. Orchids are
the oldest flowering plant with hundreds of species
each with its own pollinating insect. The future is
a salesman. We were looking for mushrooms.
History is just one path. The space between a word
and here puffs out like a milkweed seed. Our lives have
their wires crossed. Everything seems short-circuited.
The shadows of stars follow us even through daylight.
March, 1859, *The Weeping Time,* when Pierce Butler
auctioned off 436 slaves not far from here. There was
a time when we could mend these broken branches.
Syria still wanders around in its cage eating itself.
That metaphor shows how little I really understand.
I don't even know what the script says. The wind
seems lost. Where are the armadillos that should
have mystified me? The island is full of them.
Everyone wants to sell someone. Don't deny it.
God grows dizzy. Our words are sprinkled over our pasts.
You have to know the difference between the sound
of a star and the sound of a planet. Which one pollinates.
This page only exists if you happen to have written it.

Clouds, Myths

At 26,000 feet the clouds look more calloused.
It should be noted that no one knows what gravity is
and many theories about why a plane stays in the air.
These are the kinds of reality we once called myth
or superstition. Maybe we need our myths to blind
us the way volcanic ash cloud can blind a pilot's view.
Pliny said you can cure a scorpion sting by mixing
its ashes in your wine. Also, magpies that feed on
acorns will learn to speak. At least that's what some
medieval tapestries suggest. And the unicorns on those
tapestries may stand for Christ. Marco Polo thought
the rhino was a unicorn. In one legend a unicorn's tears
heal a maiden's heart. At 20,000 feet the lightning
flashes buried in the clouds are either artillery flashes
or the thunderbolts of Zeus. Or our own galaxy headed
for another galaxy. Each millennium the planets create
a new geometry of the sky. No one will ever decipher
the tapestry of our hearts. It's like those cold war maps
showing roads that don't exist to confuse some imagined
enemy. The ponds below us are strung out like mythic
tracks, perhaps of Anteros, the god of requited love,
which is all we can hope for. This is our final approach—
everyone on board dreaming of unicorns or gorgons,
the reality we can't have or the one we don't want.

Rock Birds

No wonder the first people here believed we came from stone.
What these birds were waiting for was the day we would return.
The lizards wrap themselves in light. The wind whispers into
the ear of the sky. The shadows have a purpose we'll never
decipher. Nevertheless, these birds invite us to speak to them.
At night these rocks will be iced with light. The question
they would answer is why they left the air. They are no longer
surprised by what we have tried to carve into history.
Sometimes our words hold an idea for a few moments before
the sand claims it. The mind shivers at this thought. Reality
seems like a provocation. Nevertheless, these birds, they are
silent to say whatever has been wearing us down, carving us
into shapes we could never imagine, never refuse to believe.

The Wall

AT THE LENNON WALL, PRAGUE

The wall was always within us. We have to write it
until it opens. There's a girl—is she writing or drawing—
what happens to that space when she leaves? Between
'girl' and 'leaves' I had written the expression on her
face, erased it, let it settle in another space that has
nothing to do with her. What comes after a wall is
a dream of wall, a question that means the soul is all sky.
Only Daniel knew what the writing really meant.
The sky seduces the unknown. It's the heart's proof.
In this way it is easy to become the shadow of a bird.
If you have read this far you will believe this.

Turkeys Lined Up on the Fence

CHICKAMAUGA BATTLEFIELD, GEORGIA

There's always one word that questions the others.
Just as in a universe made of elegant laws we are
mere flaws or breaks in that symmetry. The laws
of gravity arise from the God particle. We have to
trust so much simply to get through the day. We are
always on the fence between one word and another.
We can almost say the thunder, almost feel the moon's
ancient scars. We beat our wings against an invisible air
while each word keeps migrating towards its difficult end.

Crowded Parchment Mushrooms

They gather like ideas we haven't written on yet.
Spanish priests thought the Aztecs used mushrooms
to communicate with devils. Here they just help
decompose wood. Each one is a chapter heading
for our unplotted days. Today's subject keeps
changing. Legends, superstitions, histories,
it's hard to keep them separate. Like the story
of the Cherokee boy who escaped the Trail of Tears
by covering himself with lichens, moss and mushrooms
which he became, his name forever lost or else
spoken in the originless hum and buzz of insects.
These are whole sentences we haven't learned to pronounce.

for Marvin Bell

Cliff Dwellers

They built their language into the rocks. It is not
who first said *tree* or *sky* but what they saw, seeing it.
For tree it might be *sky,* or *ladder* or *Spirit.* They could
climb down on ladders into their idea of the earth
where the sky opened up, which was Spirit. Because
the earth is so much older than we know, we are not
the reason. It's a truth we stumble over. Some feelings
prove to be too primordial for thought. Words are bait.
What gets expressed is the meaning of our words, not
the things they stand for. And what will we leave , then,
but these few words whose meanings will have changed.

Hourglass

All that's left of history is disposition, as Lorenzetti knew,

his *Temperance* holding an hourglass as if to show

a way of practicing death again and again. We were

brought here to be taken away, she says. Did the shore

provoke the wave? the broken branch the wind?

Beside the abandoned house a rusted swing set

with no swings. We try to position ourselves inside

the narrow *now*, away from acid throwing terrorists,

Mali rebels, and assault rifles next door. Promise

gives way to a simple measure of what is not. The hunched

woman at the checkout, she knows. Still, the water meter

gets read, the car filled, the groceries bought, while

our unlived lives sift back and forth through time.

Faith

The first people knew that the soul of everything glows at night.
Brother Sun, Sister Moon, prayed Francis. The mountains skipped,
the sea fled, sang David. Why, then, do our own beliefs scatter
like tumbleweed? Light cuts itself on cactus. Words stain
our lips. Beyond the lid of darkness Cochise's twisted canyons
work their disguise. You can hear the mule deer forage out of sight.
You can read their signs when the language of night becomes
the many languages of morning. You can believe in your own soul
when the seeds of your heart grow, and the dark recedes.

for Amy & Daryl

Sacrificial Table

'STONEHENGE,' SALEM, NEW HAMPSHIRE

There are rituals we don't understand trapped in stone.
This is something that has nothing to do with words.
It is pure seeing. The beetle that just slipped into
a crack doesn't have to remember the past. It doesn't
care that a sea covered this space before this space
occurred to anyone. There are secret lakes and cities
buried beneath the Sahara. In the future someone will
exhume us. Or twenty years later you suddenly realize
that you misunderstood what she said, and how
you hurt her. Our dreams are a kind of rain bucket
for our pasts. Who could read them later on? As for me,
I will be buried with a book, maybe *The Imitation of Christ,*
or Jefferson's *Bible,* or Twain's, but there will be only
crumbled flakes of their mysteries gone back to the pulp
it came from, unreadable and unknowable as any of us.

The Word for That

ANGHIARI, ITALY

The trees are tempted. The moon is gagged.
Not everyone can live alone. On the *via dei Sette Ponti*
above Arezzo I tasted the light. What wasn't
to love? I thought the pollen were butterflies.
I discovered what della Francesca's Adam was keeping
secret as he watched his own burial. Their souls still
slither behind the paint. What does the river mean
by refusing reflections under *Ponte Buriano?*
Will the road correct itself? Will the wind believe
in itself once again? I am following the path
of some Roman legion. Tuscany is my fresco.
Everyone is his own saint. One sky sails behind
another sky. Stars pile up. Even the cinghiale have
their dreams. I can't remember the word for them.
I am writing you from James Wright's Anghiari.
It's true I am brooding because the statues are hungry.
They no longer know what they mean. Do we?
Even now the soul finds another workshop.
I meant the moon is a rudder with no boat.
I meant the trees were snares. Adam looked lonely.
I've settled into Castiglion Fibocchi to wait.
At least there is fruit on the table. At least
the sky blinks. Jupiter keeps tempting the moon.
Someone else will have to close our eyes.

for Tomaž Šalamun

ACKNOWLEDGMENTS

I would like to express my gratitude to The University of Tennessee at Chattanooga for the sabbatical that provided the time to complete this book. Special thanks to Deborah Brown & Barbara Carlson for their help in preparing the manuscript. I would also like to thank the following publications where these poems first appeared:

Asheville Poetry Review

Clouds, Myths; Flood Stage; Desperate Note from Byron's Place in Lerici

BODY

Škocjan, Slovenia; The Bone Church; The Word for That;
Ruins; The Wall; Bird; Lidice; Shorelines; Tank Traps

Ecotone

Identity; The Voices

Poems and Plays

Vultures; Torture; Numbers; The Trail; The Eyes

Cortland Review

The Beach; Volunteers; Soundings

Numero Cinq

Butterflies; The Chair in the Forest; Rock Birds; Not Said; Fog

Cutthroat

Hourglass; The Dancing Building, Prague; Rapids; Faith in Romania;
Cumberland Island; Roots; Turkeys on the Fence; Faith

RICHARD JACKSON teaches at the University of Tennessee at Chattanooga and is a frequent lecturer at the MFA writing seminars at Vermont College, University of Iowa Summer Writers' Festival, Yale Writers Conference, and the Prague Summer Program. He is the author of twelve previous books of poems most recently, *Out of Place,* and *Resonance* (Eric Hofer Award. He has also published two books of translations, *Last Voyage: The Poems of Giovanni Pascoli* from Italian (2010) and Alexandar Persolja's *Journey of the Sun* from Slovene (2008). He is also the author of two critical books, *Acts of Mind: Conversations with American Poets* (Choice Award) and *Dismantling Time in Contemporary Poetry* (Agee Award Winner), and has edited two anthologies of Slovene poetry, two Slovene poetry books, as well as the journal *Poetry Miscellany.* His work has been translated into fifteen languages including a Slovene edition in 1998 and Spanish edition of *Resonance* (*Resonanacia,* Barcelona in 2014), and has appeared in *The Best American Poems,* five Pushcart anthologies, and several other collections. He has been awarded the *Order of Freedom Medal* by the President of Slovenia for literary and humanitarian work in the Balkans, and has been named a Guggenheim Fellow, Fulbright Fellow, Witter-Bynner Fellow, a National Endowment for the Arts Fellow, a National Endowment for the Humanities Fellow, and has lectured & given readings at dozens of universities & conferences here & abroad. In 2009 he won the Association of Writers & Writing Programs' George Garret National Award for Teaching & Arts Advocacy.

THE MAXINE KUMIN PRIZE IN POETRY

Maxine Kumin came to prominence as one of a generation of women poets who extended the boundaries of poetry, addressing areas of female experience which had not previously been written about. A Pulitzer Prize-winning poet, her spare, deceptively simple lines explored some of the most complex aspects of human existence—birth and death, evanescence and renewal, and the events large and small conjoining them all. An enduring presence in American poetry, Maxine Kumin's career spanned over half a century. She was the recipient of prestigious awards such as the Pulitzer Prize, the Ruth Lilly Poetry Prize, and an American Academy and Institute of Arts and Letters Award. She was the poetry consultant for the Library of Congress in 1981–1982, and taught at many of the country's most prestigious universities, including Massachusetts Institute of Technology, Princeton, and Columbia. She was a frequent faculty member at the Bread Loaf Writers' Conference and a beloved mentor & friend to younger poets & writers. She lived in Warner, New Hampshire and died in 2014. The Maxine Kumin Prize in Poetry is a tribute developed during C&R Press's first open poetry reading period in December 2013 during the last weeks of her life.